All About Turkeys

Denzel Carter

Rosen REAL READERS

Rosen Classroom™
New York

A turkey is a big bird.

A turkey has feathers.

A turkey lives on a farm.

They live in forests, too.

Female turkeys lay eggs.

Babies hatch from the eggs.

Words To Know

baby

eggs

feathers

turkey